50 Vanilla Baked Dishes for Home

By: Kelly Johnson

Table of Contents

- Vanilla Cake
- Vanilla Cupcakes
- Vanilla Cookies
- Vanilla Pudding Cake
- Vanilla Bean Cheesecake
- Vanilla Bean Muffins
- Vanilla Shortbread
- Vanilla Scones
- Vanilla Churros
- Vanilla Bean Pound Cake
- Vanilla Soufflé
- Vanilla Bean Eclairs
- Vanilla Bean Ice Cream Cake
- Vanilla Cream Puffs
- Vanilla Custard Tarts
- Vanilla Macarons
- Vanilla Bean Doughnuts
- Vanilla Cinnamon Rolls
- Vanilla Bundt Cake

- Vanilla Waffles
- Vanilla Brioche
- Vanilla Rice Pudding
- Vanilla Fudge Bars
- Vanilla Bean Brownies
- Vanilla Almond Cake
- Vanilla Panna Cotta Cake
- Vanilla Sugar Cookies
- Vanilla Bean Bars
- Vanilla Sourdough Cake
- Vanilla Flan
- Vanilla Pudding Pie
- Vanilla Cake Roll
- Vanilla Granola Bars
- Vanilla Chiffon Cake
- Vanilla Biscotti
- Vanilla Poppy Seed Cake
- Vanilla Bean Biscuits
- Vanilla Macadamia Cookies
- Vanilla Bean Tiramisu
- Vanilla Puff Pastry Twists

- Vanilla and Honey Loaf
- Vanilla Oatmeal Cookies
- Vanilla Marble Cake
- Vanilla Torte
- Vanilla Raspberry Bars
- Vanilla Yogurt Cake
- Vanilla Latte Muffins
- Vanilla and Strawberry Cupcakes
- Vanilla Spice Cake
- Vanilla Bean Madeleines

Vanilla Cake

Ingredients:

- 2½ cups (315g) all-purpose flour
- 1 tbsp baking powder
- ½ tsp salt
- 1 cup (225g) unsalted butter, softened
- 2 cups (400g) sugar
- 4 large eggs
- 1 tbsp vanilla extract
- 1 cup (240ml) milk

Instructions:

1. Preheat oven to 350°F (175°C). Grease and flour two 9-inch cake pans.
2. Mix flour, baking powder, and salt together.
3. Beat butter and sugar until light and fluffy.
4. Add eggs one at a time, then mix in vanilla.
5. Gradually add dry ingredients alternately with milk, mixing until smooth.
6. Divide batter between the pans and bake for 25-30 minutes, until a toothpick comes out clean.

Vanilla Cupcakes

Ingredients:

- 1½ cups (190g) all-purpose flour
- 1 tsp baking powder
- ½ tsp baking soda
- ½ tsp salt
- 1 cup (225g) unsalted butter, softened
- 1 cup (200g) sugar
- 2 eggs
- 1 tbsp vanilla extract
- ½ cup (120ml) milk

Instructions:

1. Preheat oven to 350°F (175°C). Line a muffin tin with cupcake liners.
2. Mix flour, baking powder, baking soda, and salt together.
3. Beat butter and sugar until light and fluffy.
4. Add eggs one at a time, then stir in vanilla.
5. Gradually add the dry ingredients alternately with milk.
6. Fill cupcake liners two-thirds full and bake for 18-20 minutes.

Vanilla Cookies

Ingredients:

- 1½ cups (190g) all-purpose flour
- ½ tsp baking soda
- ½ tsp salt
- ½ cup (115g) unsalted butter, softened
- 1 cup (200g) sugar
- 1 tsp vanilla extract
- 1 egg

Instructions:

1. Preheat oven to 350°F (175°C). Line a baking sheet with parchment paper.
2. Mix flour, baking soda, and salt in a bowl.
3. Cream butter and sugar until fluffy, then beat in the egg and vanilla.
4. Gradually add dry ingredients and mix until combined.
5. Drop spoonfuls of dough onto the baking sheet and bake for 8-10 minutes.

Vanilla Pudding Cake

Ingredients:

- 1 cup (200g) sugar
- ½ cup (60g) all-purpose flour
- 2 cups (480ml) milk
- 2 tsp vanilla extract
- 4 large eggs, separated
- 1 tbsp butter, melted

Instructions:

1. Preheat oven to 350°F (175°C). Grease a baking dish.
2. Mix sugar, flour, and milk together in a saucepan. Cook over medium heat, stirring constantly, until thickened.
3. Remove from heat and add vanilla and butter.
4. Beat egg yolks and stir into the mixture.
5. Whisk egg whites until stiff peaks form, then fold them into the batter.
6. Pour into the dish and bake for 30-35 minutes until golden.

Vanilla Bean Cheesecake

Ingredients:

- 2 cups (250g) graham cracker crumbs
- ¼ cup (50g) sugar
- ½ cup (115g) butter, melted
- 3 cups (675g) cream cheese, softened
- 1 cup (200g) sugar
- 3 large eggs
- 1 vanilla bean, scraped
- 1 tsp vanilla extract

Instructions:

1. Preheat oven to 325°F (160°C). Grease a springform pan.
2. Mix graham cracker crumbs, sugar, and butter, then press into the bottom of the pan.
3. Beat cream cheese and sugar until smooth.
4. Add eggs, one at a time, mixing in between.
5. Stir in vanilla bean seeds and vanilla extract.
6. Pour into the pan and bake for 55-60 minutes. Let cool, then refrigerate for at least 4 hours.

Vanilla Bean Muffins

Ingredients:

- 1½ cups (190g) all-purpose flour
- ½ cup (100g) sugar
- 1 tsp baking powder
- ½ tsp baking soda
- ½ tsp salt
- 1 cup (240ml) milk
- ½ cup (115g) unsalted butter, melted
- 1 egg
- 1 vanilla bean, scraped

Instructions:

1. Preheat oven to 350°F (175°C). Line a muffin tin with paper liners.
2. Mix dry ingredients together.
3. Beat wet ingredients together, then stir in the dry ingredients.
4. Fold in vanilla bean seeds.
5. Fill muffin cups two-thirds full and bake for 18-20 minutes.

Vanilla Shortbread

Ingredients:

- 1½ cups (190g) all-purpose flour
- ½ cup (50g) powdered sugar
- ½ tsp salt
- 1 cup (225g) unsalted butter, softened
- 1 tsp vanilla extract

Instructions:

1. Preheat oven to 325°F (165°C). Line a baking sheet with parchment paper.
2. Cream butter and powdered sugar until fluffy.
3. Gradually add flour and salt, mixing until combined.
4. Stir in vanilla extract.
5. Roll dough into a log and slice into rounds.
6. Bake for 15-20 minutes until lightly golden.

Vanilla Scones

Ingredients:

- 2 cups (250g) all-purpose flour
- 1/3 cup (60g) sugar
- 1 tbsp baking powder
- ½ tsp salt
- ½ cup (115g) cold butter, cubed
- 2/3 cup (160ml) milk
- 1 tsp vanilla extract

Instructions:

1. Preheat oven to 375°F (190°C). Line a baking sheet with parchment paper.
2. Mix flour, sugar, baking powder, and salt.
3. Cut in the butter until the mixture resembles coarse crumbs.
4. Stir in milk and vanilla, then form dough into a ball.
5. Roll out dough and cut into wedges.
6. Bake for 15-20 minutes until golden.

Vanilla Churros

Ingredients:

- 1 cup (240ml) water
- 2 tbsp sugar
- 1 tsp vanilla extract
- 1 cup (125g) all-purpose flour
- ¼ tsp salt
- 2 tbsp unsalted butter
- 2 eggs
- Vegetable oil for frying
- ½ cup (100g) sugar, for coating

Instructions:

1. Heat water, sugar, vanilla, and butter in a pan until boiling.
2. Stir in flour and salt, then cook until dough forms a ball.
3. Remove from heat and beat in eggs one at a time.
4. Heat oil in a pan for frying. Pipe dough into hot oil and fry until golden.
5. Drain on paper towels and coat with sugar.

Vanilla Bean Pound Cake

Ingredients:

- 2 cups (250g) all-purpose flour
- 1½ tsp baking powder
- ¼ tsp salt
- 1 cup (225g) unsalted butter, softened
- 2 cups (400g) sugar
- 4 large eggs
- 1 vanilla bean, scraped
- 1 tsp vanilla extract
- 1 cup (240ml) milk

Instructions:

1. Preheat oven to 350°F (175°C). Grease and flour a loaf pan.
2. Beat butter and sugar until light and fluffy.
3. Add eggs, one at a time, mixing in between.
4. Stir in vanilla bean seeds, vanilla extract, and dry ingredients alternately with milk.
5. Pour into the pan and bake for 60-70 minutes.

Vanilla Soufflé

Ingredients:

- 4 large eggs, separated
- 1 cup (240ml) milk
- 1 tbsp vanilla extract
- 3 tbsp sugar
- 1 tbsp all-purpose flour
- ¼ tsp salt
- 1 tbsp unsalted butter, for greasing
- ¼ cup (30g) powdered sugar, for dusting

Instructions:

1. Preheat oven to 375°F (190°C). Grease soufflé dishes with butter.
2. Heat milk in a saucepan over medium heat.
3. In a separate bowl, whisk egg yolks, sugar, and flour until smooth.
4. Gradually add hot milk to the egg mixture, whisking constantly.
5. Pour mixture back into the saucepan and cook over low heat until thickened.
6. Stir in vanilla extract and remove from heat.
7. Beat egg whites until stiff peaks form, then fold into the mixture.
8. Pour into soufflé dishes and bake for 20-25 minutes. Dust with powdered sugar before serving.

Vanilla Bean Éclairs

Ingredients:

- 1 cup (240ml) water
- 1 cup (125g) all-purpose flour
- ½ cup (115g) unsalted butter
- 4 large eggs
- 1 tsp vanilla extract
- 2 cups (480ml) heavy cream
- ¼ cup (50g) sugar
- 1 vanilla bean, scraped

Instructions:

1. Preheat oven to 400°F (200°C). Line a baking sheet with parchment paper.
2. In a saucepan, bring water and butter to a boil.
3. Stir in flour until smooth, then remove from heat and add eggs one at a time.
4. Pipe dough into long strips on the baking sheet and bake for 20-25 minutes.
5. For the filling, beat heavy cream, sugar, and vanilla bean seeds until stiff peaks form.
6. Once éclairs are cooled, slice them open and fill with the vanilla cream.

Vanilla Bean Ice Cream Cake

Ingredients:

- 1 box (10-12 oz) graham crackers, crushed
- 3 tbsp sugar
- 6 tbsp (90g) unsalted butter, melted
- 1 quart (960ml) vanilla bean ice cream, softened
- 1 pint (480ml) heavy cream
- 1 tsp vanilla extract
- 1 cup (200g) sugar

Instructions:

1. Preheat oven to 350°F (175°C).
2. Mix graham cracker crumbs, sugar, and melted butter, then press into the bottom of a springform pan.
3. Bake for 10-12 minutes and cool completely.
4. Whip cream with sugar and vanilla until stiff peaks form.
5. Layer softened vanilla bean ice cream over the cooled crust, then top with whipped cream.
6. Freeze for 4-6 hours until firm.

Vanilla Cream Puffs

Ingredients:

- 1 cup (240ml) water
- ½ cup (115g) unsalted butter
- 1 cup (125g) all-purpose flour
- 4 large eggs
- 1½ cups (360ml) heavy cream
- 2 tbsp powdered sugar
- 1 tsp vanilla extract

Instructions:

1. Preheat oven to 400°F (200°C). Line a baking sheet with parchment paper.
2. Bring water and butter to a boil, then stir in flour until the dough forms a ball.
3. Remove from heat and add eggs one at a time, mixing well between each.
4. Pipe dough onto the baking sheet and bake for 20-25 minutes.
5. Whip heavy cream, powdered sugar, and vanilla until stiff peaks form.
6. Once puffs are cooled, slice open and fill with whipped cream.

Vanilla Custard Tarts

Ingredients:

- 1 package tart shells (store-bought or homemade)
- 1¾ cups (420ml) milk
- 3 large egg yolks
- 1/3 cup (60g) sugar
- 1 tbsp cornstarch
- 1 tsp vanilla extract

Instructions:

1. Preheat oven to 350°F (175°C).
2. Bake tart shells according to package instructions and allow to cool.
3. In a saucepan, heat milk over medium heat.
4. In a bowl, whisk together egg yolks, sugar, cornstarch, and vanilla.
5. Gradually add hot milk to egg mixture, whisking constantly.
6. Return to the saucepan and cook over low heat until thickened.
7. Pour custard into tart shells and chill for 2 hours.

Vanilla Macarons

Ingredients:

- 1 cup (100g) powdered sugar
- ½ cup (50g) almond flour
- 2 large egg whites
- ¼ cup (50g) granulated sugar
- 1 tsp vanilla extract
- ½ cup (120g) butter, softened
- 1 cup (120g) powdered sugar (for buttercream)

Instructions:

1. Preheat oven to 300°F (150°C). Line a baking sheet with parchment paper.
2. Sift together powdered sugar and almond flour.
3. Beat egg whites until stiff peaks form, then gradually add granulated sugar.
4. Fold in almond mixture and vanilla extract.
5. Pipe onto the baking sheet and bake for 18-20 minutes.
6. For buttercream, beat butter and powdered sugar until fluffy.
7. Sandwich macarons with buttercream and refrigerate for 24 hours before serving.

Vanilla Bean Doughnuts

Ingredients:

- 1½ cups (190g) all-purpose flour
- ¾ cup (150g) sugar
- 1 tsp baking powder
- ¼ tsp salt
- 1 tsp vanilla extract
- 1 vanilla bean, scraped
- 2 eggs
- 1 cup (240ml) buttermilk
- ¼ cup (60g) unsalted butter, melted

Instructions:

1. Preheat oven to 350°F (175°C). Grease a doughnut pan.
2. Mix dry ingredients in a bowl.
3. In another bowl, whisk eggs, buttermilk, vanilla, and butter.
4. Gradually add wet ingredients to dry ingredients and mix until smooth.
5. Pour batter into the doughnut pan and bake for 12-15 minutes.

Vanilla Cinnamon Rolls

Ingredients:

- 1 package (2¼ tsp) active dry yeast
- ¾ cup (180ml) warm milk
- ¼ cup (50g) sugar
- ½ cup (115g) butter, softened
- 4 cups (500g) all-purpose flour
- 1 tsp salt
- 2 eggs
- 1 tbsp cinnamon
- ½ cup (100g) brown sugar

Instructions:

1. Preheat oven to 350°F (175°C). Grease a baking dish.
2. Combine yeast, warm milk, and sugar, then let sit for 5 minutes.
3. Mix butter, flour, salt, and eggs. Add yeast mixture and knead until smooth.
4. Let rise for 1 hour.
5. Roll dough into a rectangle, spread with butter, cinnamon, and brown sugar.
6. Roll up dough, slice, and bake for 25-30 minutes.

Vanilla Bundt Cake

Ingredients:

- 2½ cups (315g) all-purpose flour
- 1½ tsp baking powder
- ¼ tsp salt
- 1 cup (225g) unsalted butter, softened
- 2 cups (400g) sugar
- 4 large eggs
- 1 tbsp vanilla extract
- 1 cup (240ml) milk

Instructions:

1. Preheat oven to 350°F (175°C). Grease and flour a Bundt pan.
2. Mix flour, baking powder, and salt.
3. Beat butter and sugar until light and fluffy, then add eggs one at a time.
4. Stir in vanilla and add dry ingredients alternately with milk.
5. Pour into the pan and bake for 45-50 minutes.

Vanilla Waffles

Ingredients:

- 2 cups (250g) all-purpose flour
- 2 tbsp sugar
- 1 tbsp baking powder
- ¼ tsp salt
- 2 large eggs
- 1 cup (240ml) milk
- 1 tsp vanilla extract
- ¼ cup (60g) unsalted butter, melted

Instructions:

1. Preheat waffle iron.
2. Mix dry ingredients together.
3. Whisk eggs, milk, vanilla, and butter in another bowl.
4. Add wet ingredients to dry and stir until smooth.
5. Cook waffles according to waffle iron instructions and serve hot.

Vanilla Rice Pudding

Ingredients:

- 1 cup (200g) Arborio rice
- 4 cups (960ml) milk
- 1/2 cup (100g) sugar
- 1 tsp vanilla extract
- 1 cinnamon stick (optional)
- Pinch of salt

Instructions:

1. In a medium saucepan, combine rice, milk, sugar, and salt.
2. Bring to a gentle boil over medium heat, stirring occasionally.
3. Reduce heat to low and simmer, stirring frequently, for about 20-25 minutes, or until the rice is tender and the mixture has thickened.
4. Remove from heat and stir in vanilla extract.
5. Let it cool for a few minutes before serving. Optionally, sprinkle with cinnamon before serving.

Vanilla Fudge Bars

Ingredients:

- 2 cups (300g) white chocolate chips
- 1 cup (240ml) sweetened condensed milk
- 1 tsp vanilla extract
- 1 cup (100g) chopped nuts (optional)

Instructions:

1. Line an 8x8-inch baking pan with parchment paper.
2. In a heatproof bowl, melt white chocolate chips and sweetened condensed milk over a double boiler, stirring occasionally until smooth.
3. Remove from heat and stir in vanilla extract.
4. Pour the fudge mixture into the prepared pan and spread it evenly.
5. Sprinkle nuts on top (if desired) and refrigerate for at least 2 hours until firm.
6. Cut into bars and serve.

Vanilla Bean Brownies

Ingredients:

- 1 cup (200g) sugar
- ½ cup (115g) unsalted butter, melted
- 2 large eggs
- 1 tsp vanilla extract
- 1 vanilla bean, scraped
- ½ cup (60g) all-purpose flour
- 1/3 cup (30g) cocoa powder
- ¼ tsp salt

Instructions:

1. Preheat oven to 350°F (175°C). Grease a 9x9-inch baking pan.
2. In a bowl, whisk together sugar, melted butter, eggs, vanilla extract, and vanilla bean seeds.
3. Sift in the flour, cocoa powder, and salt, and mix until just combined.
4. Pour the batter into the prepared pan and spread it evenly.
5. Bake for 20-25 minutes, or until a toothpick inserted into the center comes out clean.
6. Let cool before cutting into squares.

Vanilla Almond Cake

Ingredients:

- 1 ½ cups (190g) all-purpose flour
- 1 ½ tsp baking powder
- ½ tsp salt
- 1 cup (240ml) unsalted butter, softened
- 1 cup (200g) sugar
- 2 large eggs
- 1 tsp vanilla extract
- 1 tsp almond extract
- ½ cup (120ml) milk

Instructions:

1. Preheat oven to 350°F (175°C). Grease and flour a cake pan.
2. In a bowl, whisk together flour, baking powder, and salt.
3. Cream butter and sugar until light and fluffy. Add eggs one at a time, then vanilla and almond extracts.
4. Gradually add dry ingredients, alternating with milk, until smooth.
5. Pour the batter into the prepared pan and bake for 30-35 minutes.
6. Let cool before serving.

Vanilla Panna Cotta Cake

Ingredients:

- 1 ½ cups (360ml) heavy cream
- 1 cup (240ml) milk
- ½ cup (100g) sugar
- 2 tsp vanilla extract
- 2 tbsp gelatin powder
- 3 large eggs

Instructions:

1. In a saucepan, combine cream, milk, and sugar. Heat over medium heat, stirring until the sugar dissolves and the mixture is hot but not boiling.
2. Remove from heat and stir in vanilla extract.
3. In a small bowl, sprinkle gelatin over 2 tbsp cold water and let it bloom for 5 minutes.
4. Add the gelatin to the hot cream mixture and stir until dissolved.
5. In a separate bowl, beat eggs and gradually whisk in the warm cream mixture.
6. Pour the mixture into a greased cake pan and refrigerate for at least 4 hours until set.

Vanilla Sugar Cookies

Ingredients:

- 1 ¾ cups (220g) all-purpose flour
- 1 tsp baking soda
- ½ tsp baking powder
- ¼ tsp salt
- 1 cup (200g) sugar
- ½ cup (115g) unsalted butter, softened
- 1 large egg
- 1 tsp vanilla extract

Instructions:

1. Preheat oven to 350°F (175°C). Line a baking sheet with parchment paper.
2. In a bowl, whisk together flour, baking soda, baking powder, and salt.
3. In a separate bowl, cream butter and sugar until light and fluffy. Add the egg and vanilla extract, mixing well.
4. Gradually add the dry ingredients and mix until combined.
5. Roll the dough into small balls and place them on the baking sheet. Flatten slightly with a fork.
6. Bake for 10-12 minutes, or until the edges are golden.

Vanilla Bean Bars

Ingredients:

- 1 ½ cups (190g) all-purpose flour
- 1 tsp baking powder
- 1 tsp vanilla extract
- 1 vanilla bean, scraped
- ½ cup (115g) unsalted butter, softened
- ¾ cup (150g) sugar
- 2 large eggs
- ½ cup (120ml) milk

Instructions:

1. Preheat oven to 350°F (175°C). Grease and flour an 8x8-inch baking pan.
2. In a bowl, whisk together flour and baking powder.
3. In a separate bowl, cream butter and sugar until light and fluffy. Add eggs, one at a time, then vanilla extract and vanilla bean seeds.
4. Gradually add the dry ingredients, alternating with milk, until smooth.
5. Pour the batter into the prepared pan and bake for 25-30 minutes.
6. Let cool before cutting into bars.

Vanilla Sourdough Cake

Ingredients:

- 1 cup (240ml) sourdough starter, fed
- 1 ½ cups (190g) all-purpose flour
- 1 tsp baking powder
- 1 tsp vanilla extract
- 1/2 cup (115g) unsalted butter, softened
- 1 cup (200g) sugar
- 2 large eggs
- ½ cup (120ml) milk

Instructions:

1. Preheat oven to 350°F (175°C). Grease and flour a cake pan.
2. In a bowl, whisk together flour and baking powder.
3. Cream butter and sugar until light and fluffy. Add eggs, one at a time, followed by vanilla extract and sourdough starter.
4. Gradually add dry ingredients, alternating with milk, until smooth.
5. Pour the batter into the prepared pan and bake for 30-35 minutes, or until a toothpick comes out clean.
6. Let cool before serving.

Vanilla Flan

Ingredients:

- 1 cup (200g) sugar
- 2 tbsp water
- 1 can (14oz) sweetened condensed milk
- 1 can (12oz) evaporated milk
- 3 large eggs
- 1 tsp vanilla extract

Instructions:

1. Preheat oven to 350°F (175°C).
2. In a saucepan, heat sugar and water over medium heat until golden and caramelized.
3. Pour caramel into a round baking dish, swirling to coat the bottom.
4. In a blender, combine condensed milk, evaporated milk, eggs, and vanilla.
5. Pour mixture into the baking dish over the caramel.
6. Place dish in a larger pan filled with hot water and bake for 45-50 minutes.
7. Let cool, then refrigerate for at least 4 hours before serving.

Vanilla Pudding Pie

Ingredients:

- 1 premade graham cracker crust
- 2 cups (480ml) whole milk
- 1 package (3.4oz) vanilla pudding mix
- 1 tsp vanilla extract
- 1 cup (240ml) heavy cream, whipped
- Shaved chocolate for garnish

Instructions:

1. In a saucepan, whisk milk and pudding mix over medium heat until thickened.
2. Stir in vanilla extract and pour into the graham cracker crust.
3. Refrigerate for 4 hours or overnight until set.
4. Top with whipped cream and garnish with shaved chocolate before serving.

Vanilla Cake Roll

Ingredients:

- 1 cup (125g) all-purpose flour
- 1 tsp baking powder
- ¼ tsp salt
- 4 large eggs
- 1 cup (200g) sugar
- 1 tsp vanilla extract
- Powdered sugar for dusting

Instructions:

1. Preheat oven to 375°F (190°C). Grease and line a 15x10-inch jelly roll pan with parchment paper.
2. Whisk flour, baking powder, and salt.
3. Beat eggs and sugar until thick and pale. Stir in vanilla.
4. Fold in flour mixture and spread batter evenly on the pan.
5. Bake for 12-15 minutes, then roll cake in a clean kitchen towel dusted with powdered sugar.
6. Once cooled, unroll, spread with filling (whipped cream or frosting), and re-roll.

Vanilla Granola Bars

Ingredients:

- 2 cups (180g) rolled oats
- ½ cup (120g) honey
- ½ cup (120g) peanut butter or almond butter
- 1 tsp vanilla extract
- 1/3 cup (50g) dried fruit (raisins, cranberries, etc.)
- 1/3 cup (50g) chocolate chips

Instructions:

1. Preheat oven to 350°F (175°C).
2. In a saucepan, melt honey and peanut butter together over medium heat.
3. Stir in vanilla extract.
4. Mix oats, dried fruit, and chocolate chips in a bowl, then pour in the honey mixture and stir to combine.
5. Press mixture into a greased 9x9-inch pan.
6. Bake for 10-12 minutes, then cool before cutting into bars.

Vanilla Chiffon Cake

Ingredients:

- 2 cups (250g) all-purpose flour
- 1½ cups (300g) sugar
- 1 tsp baking powder
- 1 tsp baking soda
- ½ tsp salt
- 1 cup (240ml) vegetable oil
- 5 large eggs, separated
- 1 cup (240ml) water
- 1 tsp vanilla extract

Instructions:

1. Preheat oven to 325°F (160°C).
2. In a large bowl, combine dry ingredients.
3. Whisk together oil, egg yolks, water, and vanilla, then stir into dry ingredients.
4. Beat egg whites until stiff peaks form, then fold into the batter.
5. Pour batter into an ungreased 10-inch tube pan and bake for 55-60 minutes.
6. Invert the pan and cool for at least 1 hour before removing from the pan.

Vanilla Biscotti

Ingredients:

- 2 cups (250g) all-purpose flour
- 1 tsp baking powder
- ¼ tsp salt
- 1 cup (200g) sugar
- 2 large eggs
- 1 tsp vanilla extract
- ½ cup (60g) sliced almonds

Instructions:

1. Preheat oven to 350°F (175°C). Line a baking sheet with parchment paper.
2. Whisk together flour, baking powder, and salt.
3. Beat eggs and sugar until pale, then add vanilla.
4. Gradually stir in the flour mixture and fold in almonds.
5. Form dough into a log on the baking sheet and bake for 25-30 minutes.
6. Slice into pieces, then bake again for 10-12 minutes until golden.

Vanilla Poppy Seed Cake

Ingredients:

- 1¾ cups (220g) all-purpose flour
- 1½ tsp baking powder
- ¼ tsp salt
- 1 cup (200g) sugar
- ½ cup (120ml) milk
- ½ cup (115g) unsalted butter, softened
- 3 large eggs
- 2 tbsp poppy seeds
- 1 tsp vanilla extract

Instructions:

1. Preheat oven to 350°F (175°C). Grease and flour a loaf pan.
2. Whisk together flour, baking powder, and salt.
3. Beat butter and sugar until light, then add eggs and vanilla.
4. Add dry ingredients alternately with milk. Stir in poppy seeds.
5. Pour into the pan and bake for 45-50 minutes.
6. Let cool before slicing and serving.

Vanilla Bean Biscuits

Ingredients:

- 2 cups (250g) all-purpose flour
- 1 tbsp baking powder
- ½ tsp salt
- ¼ cup (60g) unsalted butter, cold and cubed
- 1 cup (240ml) heavy cream
- 1 vanilla bean, scraped

Instructions:

1. Preheat oven to 425°F (220°C).
2. Whisk together flour, baking powder, and salt.
3. Cut in the cold butter until the mixture resembles coarse crumbs.
4. Stir in heavy cream and vanilla bean seeds until dough forms.
5. Turn out dough on a floured surface and fold a few times to create layers.
6. Roll dough to 1-inch thickness and cut into rounds.
7. Bake for 10-12 minutes, until golden.

Vanilla Macadamia Cookies

Ingredients:

- 1½ cups (190g) all-purpose flour
- ½ tsp baking soda
- ¼ tsp salt
- ½ cup (115g) unsalted butter, softened
- ½ cup (100g) sugar
- ½ cup (100g) brown sugar
- 1 tsp vanilla extract
- 1 large egg
- 1 cup (140g) chopped macadamia nuts
- 1 cup (175g) white chocolate chips

Instructions:

1. Preheat oven to 350°F (175°C). Line a baking sheet with parchment paper.
2. Cream together butter, sugar, and brown sugar.
3. Add vanilla and egg, then stir in dry ingredients.
4. Fold in macadamia nuts and white chocolate chips.
5. Drop spoonfuls of dough onto the baking sheet and bake for 10-12 minutes.

Vanilla Bean Tiramisu

Ingredients:

- 1 package (7oz) ladyfingers
- 2 cups (480ml) heavy cream
- 1 cup (200g) sugar
- 2 tsp vanilla extract
- 1 vanilla bean, scraped
- 1 cup (240ml) strong coffee or espresso, cooled
- 1 tbsp coffee liqueur (optional)

Instructions:

1. Whip heavy cream, sugar, and vanilla until stiff peaks form.
2. Mix coffee and coffee liqueur in a shallow dish.
3. Dip ladyfingers into the coffee mixture and layer them in a dish.
4. Spread half of the whipped cream mixture over the ladyfingers, then repeat.
5. Refrigerate for at least 4 hours before serving.

Vanilla Puff Pastry Twists

Ingredients:

- 1 sheet puff pastry, thawed
- 1 tbsp sugar
- 1 tsp vanilla extract
- 1 egg (for egg wash)

Instructions:

1. Preheat oven to 375°F (190°C). Line a baking sheet with parchment paper.
2. Roll out the puff pastry sheet on a floured surface.
3. Sprinkle sugar evenly over the pastry and drizzle with vanilla extract.
4. Slice the pastry into strips and twist each strip into a spiral.
5. Beat the egg and brush over the pastry twists.
6. Bake for 12-15 minutes, or until golden brown.

Vanilla and Honey Loaf

Ingredients:

- 2 cups (250g) all-purpose flour
- 1 tsp baking powder
- ½ tsp baking soda
- ¼ tsp salt
- 1/3 cup (80ml) honey
- 1/2 cup (120ml) milk
- 1/2 cup (115g) unsalted butter, softened
- 2 large eggs
- 1 tsp vanilla extract

Instructions:

1. Preheat oven to 350°F (175°C). Grease and flour a loaf pan.
2. In a bowl, whisk together the dry ingredients.
3. In a separate bowl, cream butter and honey together until light and fluffy.
4. Add eggs, one at a time, followed by vanilla extract.
5. Gradually add the dry ingredients alternating with milk, mixing until smooth.
6. Pour the batter into the loaf pan and bake for 50-60 minutes.
7. Let cool before slicing.

Vanilla Oatmeal Cookies

Ingredients:

- 1 cup (120g) rolled oats
- ¾ cup (90g) all-purpose flour
- 1 tsp baking soda
- ½ tsp cinnamon
- ¼ tsp salt
- ½ cup (115g) unsalted butter, softened
- ½ cup (100g) brown sugar
- 1 large egg
- 1 tsp vanilla extract
- ½ cup (85g) raisins or chocolate chips

Instructions:

1. Preheat oven to 350°F (175°C). Line a baking sheet with parchment paper.
2. Whisk together oats, flour, baking soda, cinnamon, and salt.
3. Cream butter and brown sugar until fluffy. Add egg and vanilla, mixing well.
4. Gradually add dry ingredients and stir in raisins or chocolate chips.
5. Drop spoonfuls of dough onto the baking sheet and bake for 10-12 minutes.

Vanilla Marble Cake

Ingredients:

- 1¾ cups (220g) all-purpose flour
- 2 tsp baking powder
- ¼ tsp salt
- ½ cup (115g) unsalted butter, softened
- 1 cup (200g) sugar
- 3 large eggs
- 1 tsp vanilla extract
- ½ cup (120ml) milk
- 2 tbsp cocoa powder

Instructions:

1. Preheat oven to 350°F (175°C). Grease and flour an 8-inch round cake pan.
2. In a bowl, whisk flour, baking powder, and salt.
3. Cream butter and sugar until light and fluffy. Add eggs and vanilla, then mix in dry ingredients alternately with milk.
4. Divide batter in half. Stir cocoa powder into one half of the batter.
5. Spoon alternating scoops of vanilla and chocolate batter into the pan and swirl with a knife to create a marble effect.
6. Bake for 30-35 minutes. Let cool before serving.

Vanilla Torte

Ingredients:

- 2 cups (250g) all-purpose flour
- 1½ tsp baking powder
- ¼ tsp salt
- 1 cup (200g) sugar
- ½ cup (120g) unsalted butter, softened
- 4 large eggs
- 1 tsp vanilla extract
- ½ cup (120ml) milk
- 1 cup (240ml) heavy cream

Instructions:

1. Preheat oven to 350°F (175°C). Grease and line a 9-inch springform pan.
2. Whisk together flour, baking powder, and salt.
3. Cream butter and sugar until light and fluffy. Add eggs, one at a time, then vanilla.
4. Gradually add dry ingredients alternately with milk.
5. Pour the batter into the prepared pan and bake for 30-35 minutes.
6. Whip the heavy cream until stiff peaks form, then serve the torte with whipped cream on top.

Vanilla Raspberry Bars

Ingredients:

- 1¾ cups (220g) all-purpose flour
- 1 tsp baking powder
- ½ tsp salt
- ½ cup (115g) unsalted butter, softened
- 1 cup (200g) sugar
- 1 large egg
- 1 tsp vanilla extract
- 1 cup (240g) raspberry jam

Instructions:

1. Preheat oven to 350°F (175°C). Grease a 9x9-inch baking pan.
2. In a bowl, whisk together flour, baking powder, and salt.
3. Cream butter and sugar until light and fluffy. Add egg and vanilla, mixing well.
4. Gradually add dry ingredients, then spread the dough evenly in the prepared pan.
5. Spoon raspberry jam over the dough and swirl it slightly with a knife.
6. Bake for 25-30 minutes or until the top is golden. Let cool before cutting into bars.

Vanilla Yogurt Cake

Ingredients:

- 1 cup (240g) plain yogurt
- 1½ cups (190g) all-purpose flour
- 1 tsp baking powder
- 1 tsp vanilla extract
- ½ cup (115g) unsalted butter, softened
- 1 cup (200g) sugar
- 3 large eggs
- Zest of 1 lemon

Instructions:

1. Preheat oven to 350°F (175°C). Grease and flour a loaf pan.
2. In a bowl, whisk together flour and baking powder.
3. Cream butter and sugar until light and fluffy. Add eggs one at a time, then stir in vanilla and lemon zest.
4. Gradually add dry ingredients, alternating with yogurt, until smooth.
5. Pour the batter into the loaf pan and bake for 45-50 minutes, or until a toothpick comes out clean.
6. Let cool before serving.

Vanilla Latte Muffins

Ingredients:

- 1¾ cups (220g) all-purpose flour
- 1 tsp baking powder
- ½ tsp baking soda
- ½ tsp salt
- ½ cup (120ml) milk
- ¼ cup (60ml) brewed coffee, cooled
- 1 tsp vanilla extract
- 1 large egg
- 1 cup (200g) sugar
- ½ cup (115g) unsalted butter, softened

Instructions:

1. Preheat oven to 350°F (175°C). Line a muffin tin with paper liners.
2. In a bowl, whisk together flour, baking powder, baking soda, and salt.
3. In a separate bowl, combine milk, brewed coffee, vanilla, egg, and sugar.
4. Beat in butter until smooth, then add the wet ingredients to the dry ingredients.
5. Stir until just combined, then spoon the batter into the muffin cups.
6. Bake for 15-18 minutes or until a toothpick comes out clean.

Vanilla and Strawberry Cupcakes

Ingredients:

- 1 cup (120g) all-purpose flour
- 1 tsp baking powder
- ½ tsp baking soda
- ½ tsp salt
- 1/2 cup (115g) unsalted butter, softened
- 1 cup (200g) sugar
- 2 large eggs
- 1 tsp vanilla extract
- ¼ cup (60ml) milk
- ¼ cup (60g) strawberry jam

Instructions:

1. Preheat oven to 350°F (175°C). Line a muffin tin with paper liners.
2. In a bowl, whisk together flour, baking powder, baking soda, and salt.
3. In a separate bowl, cream butter and sugar until light and fluffy. Add eggs one at a time, then vanilla.
4. Gradually add dry ingredients, alternating with milk, until smooth.
5. Spoon the batter into the muffin cups and swirl in a teaspoon of strawberry jam into each cupcake.
6. Bake for 18-20 minutes, or until a toothpick comes out clean.

Vanilla Spice Cake

Ingredients:

- 2 cups (250g) all-purpose flour
- 1½ tsp baking powder
- 1 tsp cinnamon
- ½ tsp nutmeg
- ¼ tsp ground cloves
- ½ tsp salt
- 1 cup (200g) sugar
- ½ cup (120g) unsalted butter, softened
- 2 large eggs
- 1 tsp vanilla extract
- 1 cup (240ml) milk

Instructions:

1. Preheat oven to 350°F (175°C). Grease and flour a cake pan.
2. In a bowl, whisk together flour, baking powder, cinnamon, nutmeg, cloves, and salt.
3. Cream butter and sugar until light and fluffy. Add eggs one at a time, then stir in vanilla.
4. Gradually add dry ingredients, alternating with milk, until smooth.
5. Pour the batter into the prepared pan and bake for 30-35 minutes.
6. Let cool before frosting or serving.

Vanilla Bean Madeleines

Ingredients:

- 1 cup (120g) all-purpose flour
- 1 tsp baking powder
- ¼ tsp salt
- ½ cup (115g) unsalted butter, melted
- 2 large eggs
- ¾ cup (150g) sugar
- 1 tsp vanilla extract
- 1 vanilla bean, scraped
- Powdered sugar for dusting

Instructions:

1. Preheat oven to 375°F (190°C). Grease and flour madeleine pans.
2. In a bowl, whisk together flour, baking powder, and salt.
3. In a separate bowl, beat eggs and sugar until light and fluffy. Stir in melted butter, vanilla extract, and vanilla bean seeds.
4. Gradually add dry ingredients, mixing until just combined.
5. Spoon the batter into the madeleine molds and bake for 10-12 minutes, or until golden.
6. Let cool slightly, then dust with powdered sugar before serving.

www.ingramcontent.com/pod-product-compliance
Lightning Source LLC
LaVergne TN
LVHW081506060526
838201LV00056BA/2972